The Earth, the Sun and the Moon

Written by Sarah O'Neil
Series Consultant: Linda Hoyt

WorldWise®
Content-based Learning

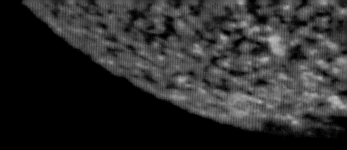

Contents

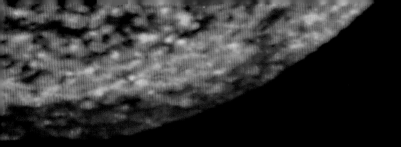

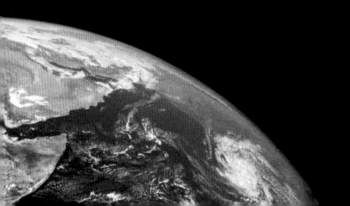

Our place in space

Do you know what this is?

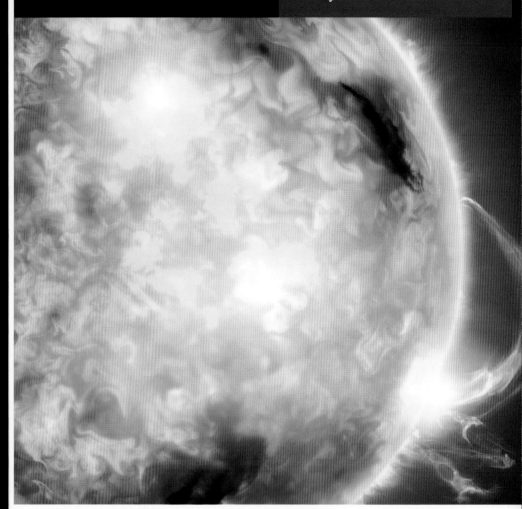

It is more than one million times bigger than Earth and the largest object in our **solar system**. It is hotter than the hottest volcano on Earth. It is the source of nearly all of the life and **energy** on our planet.

It is the sun.

Do you know what this is?

Do you know what this is?

It travels through space at over 100,000 kilometres per hour. It is the fifth biggest planet in our solar system. It is the only planet where there are known to be living things.

It is a huge rock that spins through space. It has no light of its own but shines in the sky. We see only one side of it.

It is the earth.

It is the moon.

What is the relationship between the sun, the moon and the earth?
Why do you need to know about it? This book will help you find out.

The sun: A bright star

What is the sun?

The sun is a star like the other stars we see in the sky. All stars are burning balls of gas that give off **energy** such as heat and light. It may seem that the sun is much bigger, brighter and hotter than other stars but this is only because it is much closer to us than other stars. However, the sun is about 150 million kilometres away.

▶ If the sun were the same size as a bowling ball, Earth would be no bigger than a peppercorn.

How big is the sun?

The sun may look small in the sky but it is huge compared with Earth. It is 100 times wider than Earth. One million Earths would fit inside the sun if it were hollow!

Find out more

Why is the sun so important? What would happen if the sun cooled and stopped burning?

What is the sun made of?

The sun is a ball of burning gases that shine brightly and give off heat. Although the sun is not solid like the earth, it looks like a solid ball to us. This is because gases in the centre of the sun are so dense we are able to see them.

How hot is the sun?

The sun is hottest in the centre and coolest on the surface. Temperatures on the surface of the sun vary from place to place, but they are about 5,500 degrees Celsius. In the centre of the sun, the temperature is about 14 million degrees Celsius.

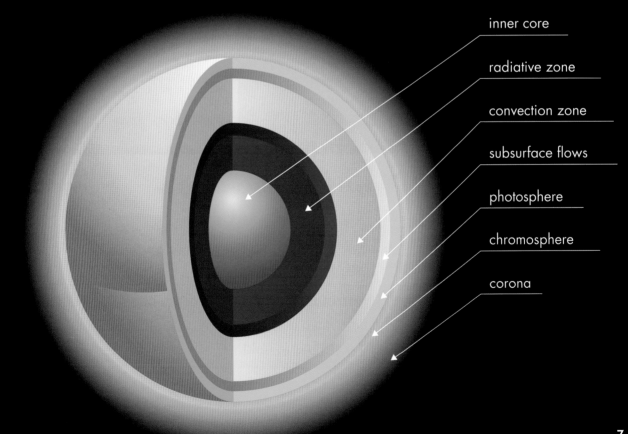

inner core

radiative zone

convection zone

subsurface flows

photosphere

chromosphere

corona

What are hot spots, sunspots and solar flares?

The surface of the sun is always changing. Some places on the surface of the sun are hotter than others. These places are called hot spots. Places that are cooler are called sunspots. Sunspots look like dark spots on the surface of the sun and usually last for a few days. Very big sunspots can last for a few weeks and can be 30 times bigger than the earth. Solar flares are huge explosions on the surface of the sun.

Try this

You can see a magnetic field by trying this experiment. Put a magnet under a piece of paper and then sprinkle iron filings over the paper. The iron filings are attracted to the lines of the magnetic field of the magnet. Try this with different-shaped magnets to see what happens.

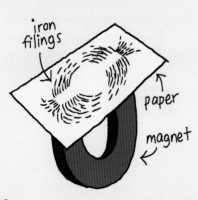

iron filings

paper

magnet

solar flare

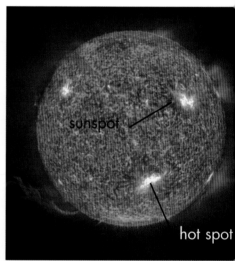

sunspot

hot spot

What is the sun's magnetic field?

The sun is a bit like a giant magnet because it has its own powerful magnetic field. This magnetic field surrounds the sun and covers our **solar system.** Magnets have a force that moves along invisible lines called a magnetic field.

 **Try this**

Build a sunspotter to observe sunspots

You will need:

- cardboard tube about 1 metre long and 15 centimetres in diameter
- cardboard box
- thin white paper
- adhesive tape
- pencils
- scissors
- aluminium foil

WARNING! WARNING!
The sun's energy is strong. Never look at the sun directly because you could seriously damage your eyes.

What to do:

1. Tape the foil to one end of the tube.

2. Make a small hole in the middle of the foil with a sharp pencil.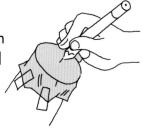

3. Tape the thin white paper to the other end of the tube.

4. Cut a hole in one side of the box to fit the tube through.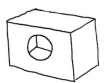

5. Cut off the other side of the box.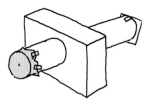

Using your sunspotter

- On a sunny day, hold the sunspotter so that the pinhole end of the tube is facing the sun. You may have to adjust the position until the image of the sun appears on the white paper.
- Trace around the image, including any dark spots. These are sunspots.
- Place a new piece of white paper on your sunspotter and repeat at other times to collect data about sunspot activity.
- How many sunspots do you see each day?

What is a solar wind?

The sun's magnetic field pushes millions of **particles** of gas through space. These particles are called plasma. Plasma is made when the extreme heat of the sun splits **atoms** of gas into particles. Plasma moves through space very quickly, and this movement is called solar wind.

What is a solar storm?

If a solar wind becomes very strong, it can become a solar storm. Although the earth's magnetic field protects us from the full force of solar storms, they can still cause damage. Satellites can be badly affected by solar storms and may need to be shut down to prevent them from being damaged. Sometimes solar storms can cause electricity supplies on Earth to suddenly become much stronger. This is called a power surge. Power surges can cause power failures when electrical wires become overheated and burn out.

▼ One effect of solar wind can be seen in the beautiful lights of the aurora borealis, which lights up the night sky with amazing colours. This happens when particles from solar wind collide with Earth's atmosphere.

Will the sun last forever?

As the sun shines, it is slowly using up the gases it is made of. This means that one day the sun will dim and become cold. But no one reading this book needs to worry because the sun is likely to burn strongly for another five million years.

How do scientists know about the sun?

Scientists continue to study the sun to learn more about what it is like and how it behaves. They use telescopes that look at the sun from both Earth and space.

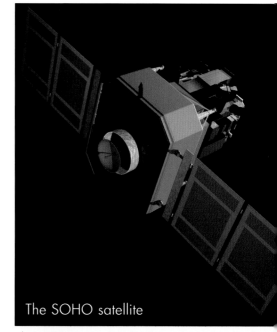

The SOHO satellite

Did you know?

In 1995, scientists sent a satellite called SOHO (Solar and Heliospheric Observatory) to **orbit** the sun. SOHO takes photographs and collects information about the sun.

Study the sun
Visit the NASA website to
see what the sun is doing today.

The earth: Our home

The sun has eight planets that move around it. We call the sun and the planets that travel around the sun the **solar system**. Earth is the fifth biggest planet in our solar system and it is the third closest planet to the sun.

Earth travels around the sun on an oval pathway called an **orbit**. Travelling at more than 100,000 kilometres per hour, Earth takes one year to complete an orbit of the sun.

Venus

Mercury

Earth

Try this

Next time you visit the ocean or a large lake, watch carefully to see what happens as a boat appears to sail over the horizon. Which part of the boat disappears first? Does the top or the bottom of the boat disappear first? How does this prove that Earth is not flat?

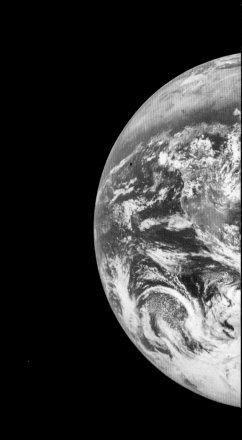

The rocky earth

If people could travel to the centre of the earth, they would move from a hard outer crust, through boiling **molten** rock, to the centre, where they would find a solid core of iron.

The crust

The surface of the earth is called the crust. The earth's crust is made up of huge rocky plates that slowly move towards or away from each other.

The mantle

Under the crust is the mantle. The mantle is so hot that some of the rock it is made from melts. This molten rock, called **magma**, sometimes pushes through weak spots in the crust. This causes volcanoes to erupt.

The core

The core at the centre of the earth has two layers: the outer core and the inner core. The outer core is made of molten iron that is moving. The inner core is made of solid iron.

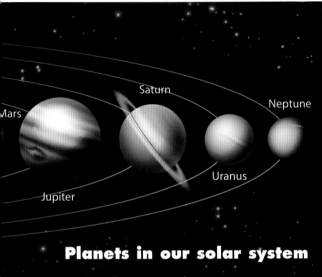

Planets in our solar system

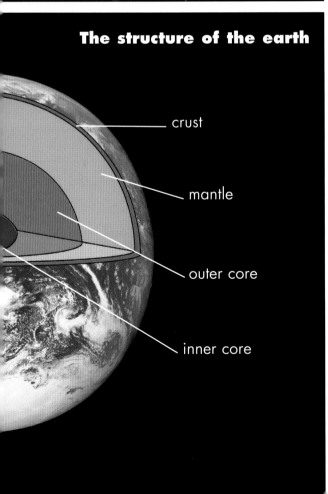

The structure of the earth

crust

mantle

outer core

inner core

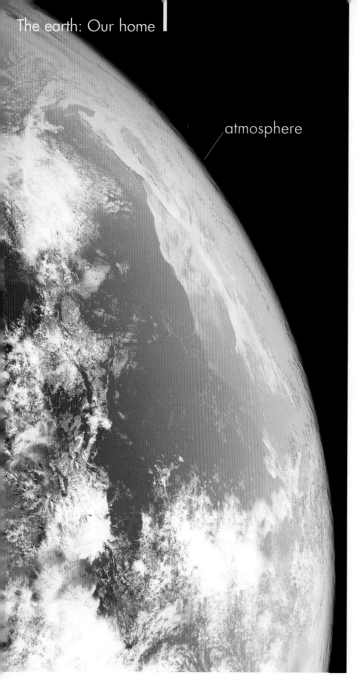

atmosphere

▲ From space, the atmosphere looks like a thin blue line around the earth.

Find out more

Imagine what it would be like as you travelled away from Earth through the different layers of the atmosphere.

The atmosphere

Earth is surrounded by a layer of gases called the atmosphere. Without the atmosphere, there would be no life on the earth. The atmosphere contains the air we need to breathe. It has four layers.

1. The lower part of the atmosphere is called the troposphere. Almost all of Earth's weather happens here. As you move up through the troposphere it gets colder.

2. The stratosphere contains a gas called ozone, which absorbs a lot of the sun's dangerous ultraviolet light. Without ozone, people would be badly sunburned after only a few minutes in the sun. It is warmer in the stratosphere than in the troposphere.

3. It is very cold in the mesosphere. The temperature can be as low as −99 degrees Celsius.

4. The thermosphere absorbs a lot of the sun's heat. Temperatures of more than 1,700 degrees Celsius have been recorded in the outer part of the thermosphere.

There is no clear place where the atmosphere finishes. It gets thinner until it reaches outer space.

Layers of the atmosphere

The atmosphere starts at the earth's surface and extends towards space for about 560 kilometres.

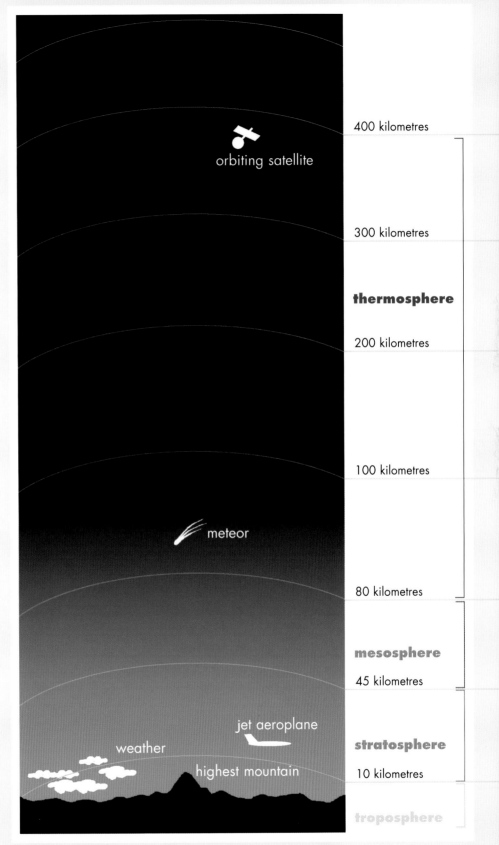

400 kilometres

300 kilometres

thermosphere

200 kilometres

100 kilometres

80 kilometres

mesosphere

45 kilometres

stratosphere

10 kilometres

troposphere

orbiting satellite

meteor

jet aeroplane

weather

highest mountain

The greenhouse effect

Earth's atmosphere protects us from the sun's extreme heat during the day. The atmosphere also traps some of the heat near the earth's surface at night when there is no heat from the sun. This is called the greenhouse effect because the atmosphere traps the sun's heat much like a greenhouse does.

Greenhouses are made from clear glass that lets in the sun's heat during the day. At night, as temperatures outside cool, some of the heat produced during the day is trapped inside the greenhouse. This keeps the plants warm and protects them.

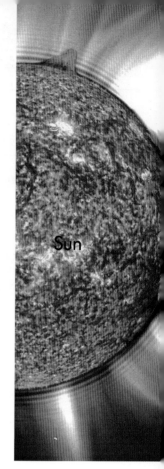

Sun

▼ As the sun shines on Earth, some of its heat is **deflected** back into space by the atmosphere. The heat that gets through the atmosphere warms the earth. After the earth has been warmed by the sun, some of the heat escapes back into space and some is trapped by the atmosphere.

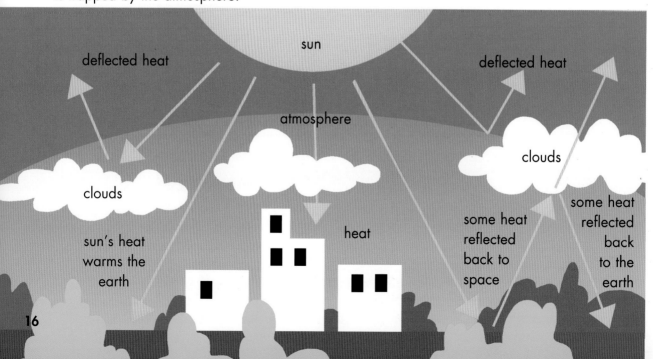

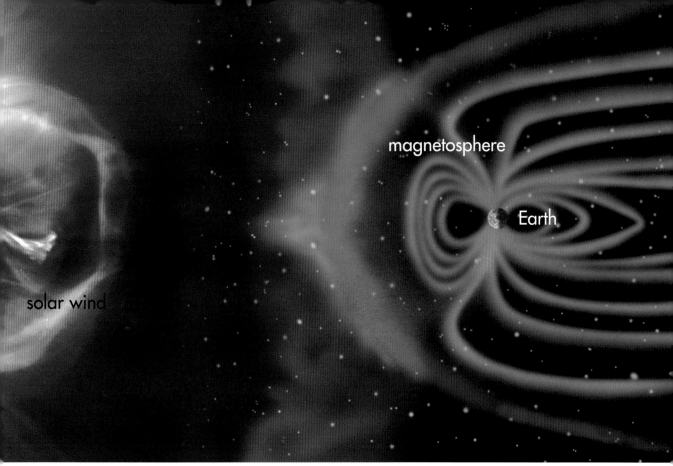

magnetosphere

Earth

solar wind

The magnetosphere

Earth is like a giant magnet. The invisible lines of its magnetic field run between the north and south of the planet. This magnetic force stretches out into space and is called the magnetosphere.

The magnetosphere protects Earth from solar wind. It pushes most of the **particles** in a solar wind to the side so that they move past the earth instead of damaging it.

When the magnetosphere deflects solar wind, it stops the gases in the atmosphere from being slowly blown away. Scientists think that without the magnetosphere it is unlikely that the earth would even have an atmosphere. This means that there would be little chance of life on Earth.

▲ Solar wind reaches speeds of well over 1,600,000 kilometres per hour as it travels past the earth. This diagram shows the magnetosphere deflecting the solar wind.

Find out more

Learn more about the earth. Visit: spaceplace.nasa.gov

The moon

The moon is a ball-shaped rock that travels around the earth. The dark and light parts that can be seen on the side of the moon are actually mountains and plains on its surface. The light areas are mountains and the dark areas are plains. Scientists have not found any evidence of life on the moon.

Where did the moon come from?

Many scientists say that the moon was created when a rock the size of Mars crashed into the earth. Pieces of rock flew back into space and gathered to form the moon. Scientists think that the moon has been **orbiting** the earth for about 4.5 billion years.

The moon does not change

The moon has no atmosphere so it has no weather. The surface of the moon has changed very little over time because there is no wind or running water to cause **erosion**. **Meteorites** hitting the moon cause changes to the moon's surface.

Moon facts
- The moon is about 380,000 kilometres from Earth.
- More than 70 spacecraft have been sent to the moon.
- Twelve astronauts have walked on the moon.
- 382 kilograms of rock and soil have been brought back from the moon for scientists to study.
- Many other planets have moons.

Phases of the moon

The moon's shape is always the same, but its appearance changes. Sometimes the moon appears to be a full circle. At other times, it appears as a thin crescent. These changes are known as the phases of the moon.

The moon does not make any of its own light. Instead it reflects sunlight. When Earth blocks some of the sunlight from reaching the moon, the moon's appearance changes.

Did you know?

Sometimes the earth's shadow blocks all or some of the sun's light from reaching the moon. This is called a lunar eclipse.

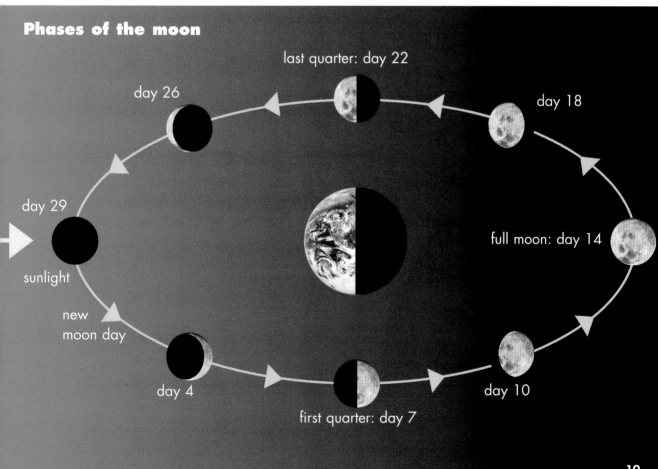

Phases of the moon

last quarter: day 22

day 26

day 18

day 29

full moon: day 14

sunlight

new moon day

day 4

day 10

first quarter: day 7

Why are the sun and moon important?

Earth would not exist without the sun. The sun is the earth's main source of **energy** and it affects all living things. Without it there would be no life on our planet.

The moon **orbits** the earth. It causes the tides in the oceans.

Sun's gravity

The sun has **gravity** that pulls the earth and other planets towards it. This pull keeps these planets moving around the sun at roughly the same distance all the time.

If the sun's gravity did not keep the earth in this orbit, the earth would fly off through space and away from the sun's heat and light.

Wind

The sun powers our weather. Heat from the sun warms air in the atmosphere, causing it to rise and move. This is why we have wind.

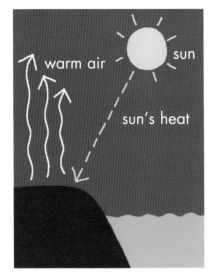 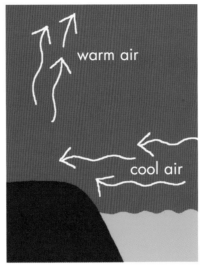 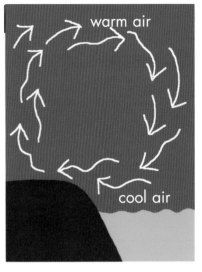

1. Sun warms land more quickly than sea. Air is warmed and rises.

2. Cooler air moves in to fill the space left by warmer air. This air movement is called wind.

3. Rising warm air cools and replaces the cold air that moved inland. Air cools and falls.

Water cycle

The sun's heat also warms water in the ocean and on the land, causing it to evaporate. This is the start of the water cycle.

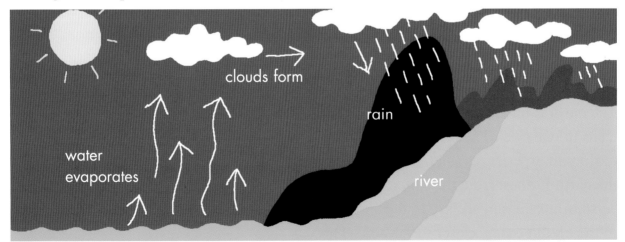

▲ The sun's heat causes water to evaporate and rise into the atmosphere. It cools in the atmosphere, again becoming a liquid that falls to the earth as rain.

21

Day and night

The earth spins around on its **axis** as it orbits the sun. This rotation brings different places on the earth into sunlight and daytime begins. As those places move away from the sunlight, night falls. We measure 24 hours as the time it takes Earth to complete a single rotation.

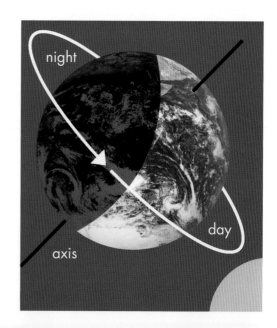

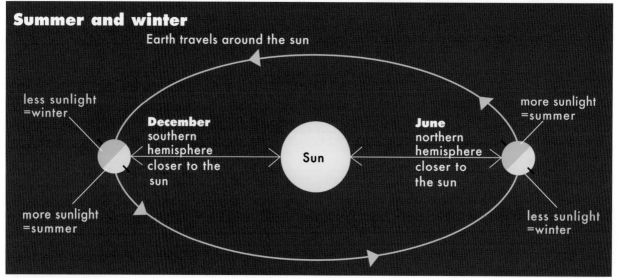

Summer and winter

Earth travels around the sun

less sunlight
=winter

December
southern
hemisphere
closer to the
sun

Sun

June
northern
hemisphere
closer to
the sun

more sunlight
=summer

more sunlight
=summer

less sunlight
=winter

Seasons

The earth is tilted on its axis, which means it leans to one side. The part of the earth closest to the sun experiences summer, and the part of the earth furthest from the sun, winter. As the earth orbits the sun each year, different parts of the earth become closer to the sun. This creates the seasons.

▲ In June, it is summer in the northern hemisphere because the northern hemisphere receives three times as much sunlight as the southern hemisphere. At this time, it is winter in the southern hemisphere. In December, the seasons are reversed.

Ocean currents

The waters of the oceans are constantly moving from one place to another. The movement of a large amount of water in one direction is called a current.

Ocean currents are caused by the sun's energy, wind movement and the way the earth spins. It is hotter at the equator because it is closer to the sun. It is cooler at the north and south poles because they are further from the sun. Because of this, the oceans are warmer closer to the equator and cooler at the poles.

When ocean water near the equator is warmed by the sun, the water rises and expands. This draws in cooler water underneath the warm water. The movement of cooler and warmer water creates currents.

Find out more

How do ocean currents affect the weather in coastal places?

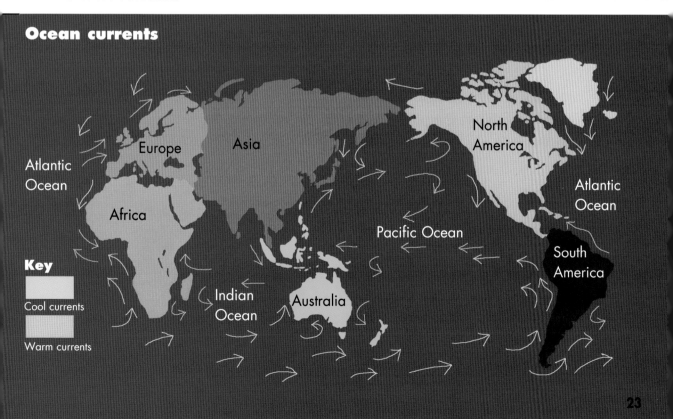

Ocean currents

Atlantic Ocean

Europe

Asia

North America

Atlantic Ocean

Africa

Pacific Ocean

South America

Key

Cool currents

Warm currents

Indian Ocean

Australia

The energy chain

The sun makes heat and light energy.

People and the sun

The sun is important in helping to provide the food we need. It helps keep us warm and healthy too, although the sun can be dangerous.

Food from the sun

Plants use the sun's energy to make food. They do this by using their leaves to turn the sun's energy into sugar. The sugar enables plants to grow. This process is called photosynthesis.

Plants use the sun's energy to make food. The sun's energy is stored in plants.

The sun's energy is stored in plants. Many animals, such as horses, cows and giraffes, eat plants. The energy stored in the plants enables the animals to live and to grow. Other animals eat the plant-eating animals, and in turn use the energy stored in their bodies to live and grow.

Animals eat plants to get energy.

People need the sun's energy for food. People eat plants and animals to get the energy they need to survive. Without the sun's energy, no living thing could survive.

People eat food from plants and animals to get energy.

A healthy amount of sunlight

People need sunlight every day to stay healthy. This is because our bodies can make vitamin D from sunlight. This vitamin helps us to build strong bones and fight infections.

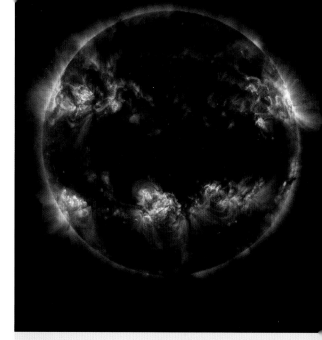

An unhealthy amount of sunlight

The sun has different types of light, such as infrared and ultraviolet light. Ultraviolet (UV) light can be very dangerous to people. In small amounts, it makes our skin tan. But too much exposure can damage our skin. UV light can also cause damage to our eyes.

By limiting the time you spend in the sun, you can help protect your skin and eyes. When you are in the sun, wear clothing that covers your skin, use sunblock and wear sunglasses that protect against UV light.

Find out more

How do people who live in places such as Iceland, where the daylight hours are very short during the winter, get enough sunlight? What happens to them if they don't get enough sun?

Electricity from the sun

Most forms of electricity rely on the sun's energy. Solar energy is the most direct way to use the sun's energy, but coal, oil and wind energy also rely on the sun to generate electricity.

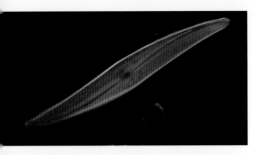

▲ Diatoms are microscopic creatures that live in water.

Solar power

Solar panels collect the energy in sunlight and turn it into electricity. This is the most direct way that the sun's energy can be used.

Oil and gas energy

Oil comes from tiny water creatures called **diatoms**. The diatoms take in energy from the sun and make an oily substance in their bodies. When the diatoms die, their bodies sink to the bottom of the ocean. Over a very long time, layers of mud, which eventually turn into rock, build up over the bodies of diatoms and press down on them. This process changes the oil in diatoms' bodies into the oil that we use to power many things, including cars and aeroplanes.

Gas given off as the oil forms is often trapped under the rock too. When people mine for this oil, this gas is released. It is called natural gas. Natural gas burns easily and is used in stoves to cook food, in heaters and as fuel for cars.

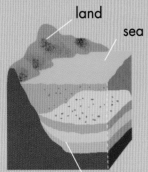

land

sea

layers of sediment form on the sea floor

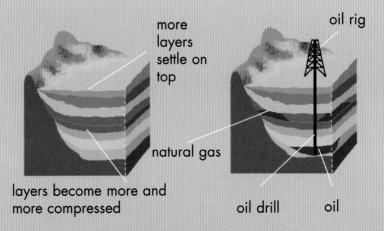

more layers settle on top

natural gas

oil rig

layers become more and more compressed

oil drill

oil

Making electricity from coal

The energy in coal originally came from the sun's energy. Millions of years ago, steamy swamps covered much of the earth. Prehistoric trees and plants lived in these swamps by taking in sunlight to make food. As the trees and plants died, they sank to the bottom of the swamps, where they formed layers of **peat**. Over many thousands of years, the layers of peat became buried under sand and rock. As the weight of the sand and rock increased, any water in the peat was squeezed out. This turned the peat into coal.

Today, people dig up coal in many parts of the world to burn it in electric power stations. The coal is burned to heat water and turn it into steam. This steam is used to operate large **generators** that make electricity.

27

The importance of the moon

Tides

As the moon spins around the earth, its gravity attracts the water in the ocean, causing the water level at the edge of the sea to rise and fall each day. This change in water level is called tides. In some places, tides can cause water levels to rise by more than three metres.

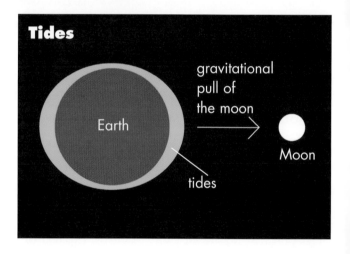

Without the moon, we would still have tides but they would be much smaller. This is because the sun has a small pull on the oceans. Changes to the tides would affect the animals that live in tidal areas. These animals rely on having some time each day underwater and some time out of water. Without tides, these animals would not survive.

 **Find out more**

When does the moon rise and set today?
What are the tides like today?
Can you see any relationship between these two things?

Scientists believe that the moon keeps the tilt of the earth's **axis** in place and stops it from wobbling on its axis. The tilt of the earth's axis spreads the sun's energy more evenly during the earth's orbit.

If the earth's axis was at a greater angle, some parts of the earth would get too much sun and become scorched, lifeless deserts, while other parts would not receive enough sunlight and become frozen wastelands.

▼ High tide

▼ Low tide

Conclusion

The sun and the moon are very important to all life on Earth. The sun gives light and warmth to our planet. And the moon moves around our planet, reflecting the sun's light onto the earth and creating the ocean tides. Without them, there would be no life on the earth.

Learning more about the relationship between the sun, the moon and the earth helps us understand more about how life on Earth is possible.

Glossary

atoms   the smallest parts of a chemical element

axis   a real or imaginary line through the middle of an object

deflected   turned aside

diatoms   types of algae that have only one cell

energy   the power to make something work

erosion   the process where the surface is worn away

generators   machines that produce electricity

gravity   the force that causes two objects to pull towards each other

magma   hot, melted rock

meteorites   pieces of rock flying through space

molten   made liquid by heat

orbit   to travel around something in a circle

particles   tiny pieces

peat   dark material made of decaying plants

solar system   the sun and all the planets and other bodies moving around it

Index

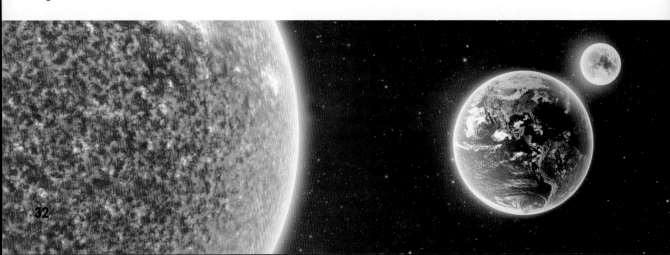